MSC

**Acknowledgements**

Educational consultant Viv Edwards, Professor of
Language in Education, University of Reading.
Illustrations by Tessa Richardson-Jones.
Photographs by Zul Mukhida except for:
p. 3b Oliver Cockell, p. 4l David Thomas, p. 4r, 5t Tim
Richardson, p. 5b John Heinrich, p. 8 Rafe Harwood, p. 9 John
Heinrich, p. 14r Graham Horner, Zul Colour Library; p. 10b
J Walter Thompson Co Ltd; p. 3t The Wildfowl & Wetlands Trust;
p. 10t Van den Bergh Foods; p. 12 copyright British Museum;
p. 15 Stephen Krasemann/NHPA; p. 17t BBC Picture Archives;
p. 17b A & B Gardener; p. 18t Bill Cooper;
p. 18b Henrietta Butler/PAL.

The author and publisher would like to thank: the staff and
pupils of Balfour Infant School, Brighton; Puma UK;
Woolworths plc; A Coombs Ltd Supermarket Pet Stores,
Brighton; Mr Hopper and 'Nelson'; Simon Hart;
PG Tips Chimp 'Samantha' courtesy of Van den Bergh Foods.

A CIP catalogue record for this book is available
from the British Library.

ISBN 0-7136-4242-4

First published 1995 by A & C Black (Publishers) Ltd
35 Bedford Row, London WC1R 4JH

© 1995 A & C Black (Publishers) Ltd

Typeset in 15/21pt Univers Medium by
Rowland Phototypesetting Ltd, Bury St Edmunds, Suffolk.

Printed in France by Partenaires

# Animals

Nicola Edwards

A&C Black · London

You can sometimes find messages on animals.

The tag hanging from this dog's collar has a message on it. The tag tells you the dog's name and where he lives.

Why do you think the dog is wearing the tag?

"NELSON"
5, MAIN. STR,
WINDHAM ON-
-SEA
SUSSEX
BN4.7PB

2

The marks on these sheep show which farm they belong to.

Can you see the rings on the legs of this goose?

The silver ring tells you what type of goose it is and where it comes from. It also tells you how old the goose is and whether it is male or female.

The other ring has a number on it. The number helps people to pick out this goose from a distance.

Here are some signs with pictures of animals on them.

GUIDE DOGS EXCEPTED

Which of the signs shows you:

that a house is protected
from burglars?
that a shop sells fish?
that toads may be crossing
the road ahead?
that guide dogs are welcome?

Look around the area where
you live. Can you find any
signs with animals on them?

Sometimes animals are linked with special occasions.

Chinese people give each new year the name of an animal. They celebrate with a street parade led by a dancing dragon.

Can you name these animals?
Which time of year do they
make you think of?

Some animals can send strong messages
just by the way they look.

How do these animals make you feel?
Which words would you use to
describe them?

Animals are often used in advertising.

This chimpanzee has been dressed up to look like a person. Does the chimp make you laugh?

Which words would you use to describe this tiger?

Can you find out what these animals are used to advertise?

Sometimes pictures of animals are used as company symbols or logos. Which animal logos can you see in this photograph?

Animals can carry a religious message.

This statue of a cat is over 2,000 years
old. The people in Ancient Egypt
who made it believed that
the cat was a goddess
called Bastet.

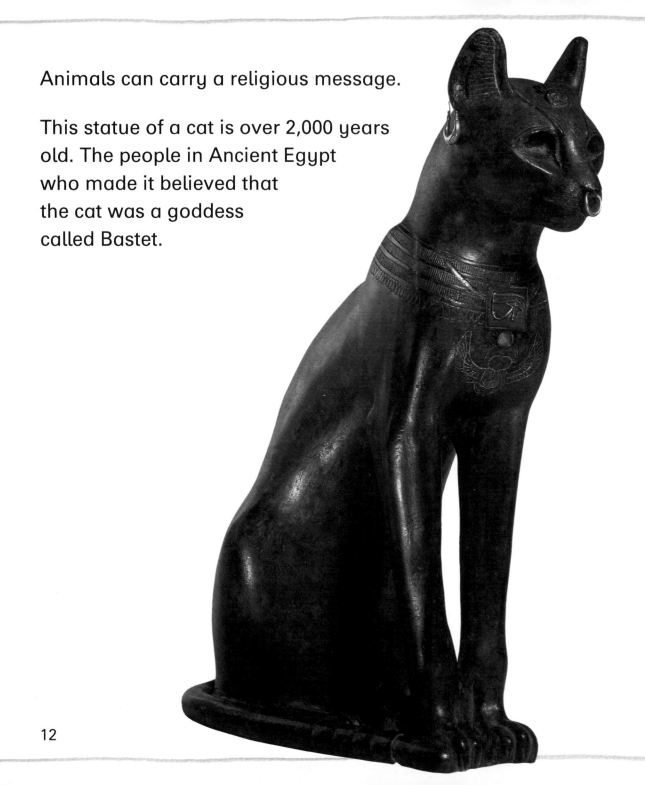

This cow lives on the streets of India where
many people follow the Hindu religion.
To Hindus, cows are sacred or holy.
Hindus do not use cows to carry loads
and do not eat beef.

Animals can give messages to each other.

This peacock is showing his tail feathers to attract a peahen.

The markings on a skunk's coat warn other animals to keep away.
The skunk will spray smelly liquid from its body at any animal that comes too close.

This cat is frightened. Its fur stands on end and it arches its back to scare off other animals.

People can teach some animals to understand them.

A dog can tell by the sound of a person's voice when it's being told off.

This shepherd is telling the sheepdog what to do by whistling and calling to it. The sheepdog will round up the flock of sheep into the pen.

This chimpanzee has been taught to use American Sign Language. When she sees the doll, she makes the sign for 'baby' with her arms.

Sometimes people dress up to look like animals and even move like them.

These ballet dancers are pretending to be swans.

Which animal do you think this actor is pretending to be?

How would you
pretend to be a lion,
a bird or a snake?
What clothes would
you wear?
How would you
move? What noise
would you make?

These children are visiting the animals in a zoo. There are messages all around them.

The signpost tells them where to find the different animals. What else are the children using to help them find their way around the zoo?

How do the children know when it is feeding time for the animals?

This sign tells the children all about cheetahs.
Some signs warn people that animals can be dangerous.

How does this sign tell the children that people can be dangerous to animals, too?

Some people keep animals as pets.

This girl has bought a hamster
from a pet shop.

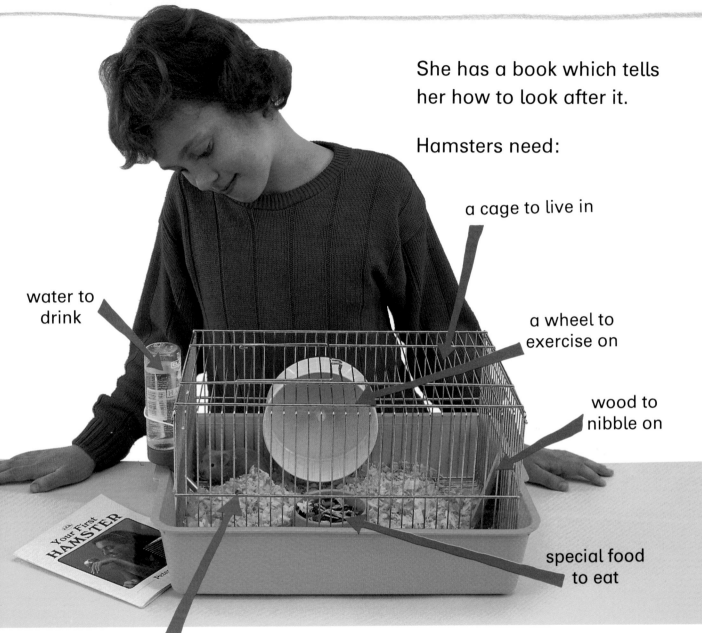

She has a book which tells her how to look after it.

Hamsters need:

a cage to live in

a wheel to exercise on

wood to nibble on

water to drink

special food to eat

wood shavings to sleep on

Your First HAMSTER

Do you have a pet? How did you find out how to look after it?

## For parents and teachers

The aim of the *Messages* series is to help build confidence in children who are just beginning to read, by encouraging them to make meaning from the different kinds of signs and symbols which surround them in their everyday lives. Here are some suggestions for follow-up activities which extend the ideas introduced in the book.

**Pages 2/3** Organise a trip to a local farm (many 'children's farms' offer information and activity packs for teachers to help make the most of your visit). Encourage the children to find out about the different ways in which animals are identified (tags on cows' ears, dye markings on sheep and goats, postcodes branded on to horses' hooves). The farm staff can give the children more information about each animal and may involve the children in helping to feed some of them.

**Pages 4/5** Take the children on a walk around the local area. You could use a camera to record the different ways in which animals feature in words and pictures on the various signs. Can the children detect differences in tone across the different messages (for example: formal, polite sticker on a shop door, informal, handwritten warning on a gate)?

**Pages 6/7** Each year in the Chinese calendar is named after one of twelve animals which recur in a chronological sequence: rat, ox, tiger, rabbit, dragon, snake, horse, sheep, monkey, rooster, dog and pig. There are several versions of the story of how the 12-year cycle came about. Each animal has its own set of characteristics. Can the children find out which animal's sign they were born under? They could extend this activity to include their family. Some children may have seen or taken part in Chinese New Year celebrations and there are several classroom-based activities (making paper dragons, lanterns and present boxes, for example) which can involve children in preparations for the festival.

**Pages 8/9** Show the children pictures of different animals and ask them to call out words which they associate with each animal. You could go on to look at how animals are used to advertise products.

**Pages 10/11** Collect pictures of animals used in newspaper and magazine advertisements (the children may have seen television advertisements which are part of the same advertising campaigns). Do any animals hold particular associations for the children which they have projected on to the products being advertised? Collect a selection of logos representing different products and companies. How many do the children recognise? Can they spot any others next time they go shopping?

**Pages 12/13** Animals form an important part of many religions. Some children may observe dietary laws such as vegetarianism, eating Halal meat or Kosher food. Animals may feature as symbols, for instance the dove of peace, or as manifestations of gods, such as Ganesha, the elephant-headed Hindu god of fortune.

**Pages 14/15** Some children may have pets and be able to describe, for instance, how their pet dog behaves towards other dogs (e.g. wagging tail, sniffing, barking). Investigate how different animals communicate with each other, with

visual signals (colours, markings), by smells and by the variety of noises that they make.

**Pages 16/17** You could invite a representative from the Guide Dogs for the Blind Association in to school to talk about how guide dogs are chosen and trained. The Association may be able to put you in touch with a local blind person who could talk to the children about how she communicates with her guide dog.

**Pages 18/19** How would the children pretend to be different animals? What sounds and movements would they make? What colour and texture of clothes would they wear? There are opportunities for mask-making and face-painting activities. The children could act out their version of a nursery rhyme or story in which animals feature, such as the tortoise and the hare or the three little pigs.

**Pages 20/21** You could arrange a trip to your local zoo. Many zoos have education departments offering resource packs for teachers with ideas on how to structure your visit and suggestions for follow-up work in the classroom. Encourage the children to notice the different ways in which information is provided about the animals, such as guide books, signposts, information plaques, taped commentaries and maps. Can they find out where in the world a particular animal is found and what it eats, using the different sources of information?

**Pages 22/23** Talk about the importance of providing the right environment for a pet to live in according to its needs (such as water, food, shelter, temperature and cleanliness). Some children may be able to talk about a pet at home which they help to look after.